God has provided this quick guide to share with those who believe that He is, and with those who don't. It is for those who have spent many nights searching for Him and those who have spent many days trying to disprove Him. And again for you who've never thought much about Him one way or another. To you all this is written. God is Real. And He wants to show you all just how to find Him.

Who is Man

and

How can he

Find God?

Who is Man
and
How can he find GOD?

an easy guide to finding The Truth

by JK Bradley

Printed in the United States of America

First Printing, 2019
ISBN: 9781077456594
Independently published

CounselInLove@outlook.com

13 14 15 16 17 18   22 21 20 19 18 17 16

God does exist.
And He's longing
for you to find Him

and when you seek Me you
will find Me when you
search for Me with your
whole heart

- God

Table of Contents

FOREWARD

This book is written for

...because God loves   you and He... desperately wanted you to know that, and to ...know how you can find Him. So get to a... quiet place, pour a glass of water, give your self about an hour, and meet God. You deserve to know the Truth of who He is and who you are in Him. Your life will never be the same once you find Him, and it's my prayer that you continue to do exceptionally wonderful things with the knowledge you are about to gain ...

God loves you.
Go find Him.
Amen.

Definition: Man

Def: man /man/ noun – A human being of either sex; A person; Created after the likeness of God; Created in the image of God; Created to have dominion over all the works of God's hands; Created a little lower than the angels; Crowned with glory and honour.[1]

Understanding Man

God allows man to be born into our nature. This nature, we put on like a glove at birth and it is laced with sin. It's nothing that anyone has to teach us. The things that we do and know as a child is who we become without any intervention from each other.[2]

We can only come to God and know Him once we realize that this ugly sin exists within us and accept that there is a better way to live. After this, we must then desire to be transformed into that better way.[3]

We might begin this transformation process on our own, with or without the intervention of another. At the point of desiring to know God and/or change our lives, one may not automatically identify this conviction, or urge, as something coming from God, because one still may not be aware of/or believe in God's existence.[4]

Just because one does not have knowledge of God, however, does not invalidate Him nor render Him unreal. In fact, it is the prodding of God that is creates the awareness within us that something needs to change! It is God's continual pursuit of man that continues to direct him in the way that he should go to be better than he is currently. God creates your desire to change toward the better.[5]

The nature of God (Holiness), which has always been, opposes the nature of man (sinfulness), which is put on at birth.[6]

The sin nature that we know from our childhood very well *might* be the thing(s) that we must fight against within our adulthood: *cruelty, stealing, sexual immorality, covetousness, etc.*[7]

One cannot definitively say that the sin nature we're born into is one we choose, but rather is an affliction upon us until we accept God's plan for us and submit to His perfected way through Jesus Christ. If one rejects God's way and decides not to turn away from their sin nature, he then is choosing to remain as he is. You can gain more insight into your particular sin nature by spending time with God and asking Him to reveal it to you. He will do so as it pleases Him.[8]

How can Man Change

It is good for a man to accept Jesus Christ and submit to His way.[9]

Parents are essential and instrumental in this exploration and molding of their children. Parents can help to expedite their child's understanding and acceptance of God and His way by interceding for them and introducing them to these truths sooner than later.[10]

Once a person has accepted their ugliness (sin) and is desirous to be better, God will present Himself to them and introduce them to The Way to Him.[11]

The way to God is through Jesus Christ (Yeshua Hamashiach), God's only Son. He is the ONLY way to the eternal God: The Heavenly Father; The sole Creator of all; The God of Abraham, Issac, and Jacob: I Am. If you have, or are, serving another god you must first renounce your participation with that false god and come to the True and Living God through Jesus Christ.[12]

Once you've accepted Jesus Christ as the only way to God, and you understand how/why, and you believe that Jesus died for your sins and that God raised Jesus from the dead because Jesus was not deserving of death (you were and Jesus took your place), then the Holy Spirit can enter into your body and live there. The Holy Spirit will help you in life to make better choices and to make the changes you need to make to please God.[13]

Rejoice! You are safe (or "saved") once this happens. And you have the ability now to repent if you sin. Repentance means "confess and don't do it anymore." You confess the ugly (sin) thing(s) that you've done and commit yourself to not doing that thing anymore.[14]

Man Reconnecting to God

It's tempting initially to think that the success in "conquering" sin is in understanding that sin displeases God. If you think this way you might handle your sin nature one of two ways when it tries to flair up in your life: 1). keep it hidden away; knowing it's there but not acting on it, or 2). acting on it privately/in secret and never speaking of it publicly. In either scenario, this will end badly because sin will win eventually in both situations if handled like this.[15]

The only way to conquer your sin nature is to give it to God. Depending on how long you've engaged in a particular sin, this could be a lengthy effort.[16]

When you see areas of darkness (hidden/secret sin) in your life and you do not give them to God, you are handling them in your own strength. Your strength is not stronger than sin.[17]

If you do not see that you are sinful and acknowledge these areas by exposing them to God, you will not be able to be changed by God. Any changes you may manage in your own strength, will be temporary.[18]

To give your sin to God you must confess it, no matter how graphic. Confess means to tell God all about it, in full detail, omitting nothing. Just as you would to a best friend, a therapist, or how it plays out in your imagination. It might be challenging the first few times, but do not suppress it and feign victory.[19]

How can Man Conquer Sin

It should be stated that man's sin is not lost on God. God is *fully* aware of who man is. However, up until the point of Salvation God has been showing you who He is, now He wants you to show Him who you are and He will remove those sinful parts of you and give you a new identity in Him through Christ Jesus. God will tell you how you should see yourself (based on who He created you to be) and He will take away how you used to see yourself. This creates perspective and history with God in your life.[20]

Man also must be clear on what God is removing and what He is replacing it with. This will help us not to succumb to those sinful ways anymore. This process highlights God's power too. His magnificent ability to cure us from any and everything! It's also an acknowledgment of our understanding before God of how debase we really are.[21]

Once we expose our sinful parts to God He will remove them from us. He will tell us why we do the things we do. And He will show us how to do things differently from then on.[22]

There might be times when we have to expose the

same sinful part of ourselves to God more than once. It's okay. Don't lose hope. Some things are deeper rooted than others. We must continue to do so and He will give us direction each time until that part is completely gone and replaced with something new that He puts inside of us.[23]

Do not let sin stay hidden in your life, whatever you do! That is always the important thing to remember. God wants to forgive you. If you confess your sin(s) God will forgive you.[24]

Man and God together

We can now tell others. Man can testify! We now know that we are tried and true people; and that God is a tried and true God! We have seen His miracles and His abilities, personally. To change a Man is miraculous, and it is something only God can do![25]

God introduces Himself to every man, personally. Even though we may not know Him to be God by terminology. God is *always* behind any thought or motive we have to do good. I believe strongly that God's presentation of Himself to us all is very early in life. As children, sometimes we listen and sometimes we don't. I believe also that our influences and nurture plays a huge part on whether or not we listen, and how keenly so.[26]

After God presents Himself to you, God might then send someone else in human form to help you understand and acknowledge what He has been doing in your life. This person may be known or unknown to you. This person may tell you something like "do you ever feel like something is leading you to do the right thing in times when you have otherwise done the wrong thing?" or "Do you know Jesus?" or any other number of things. This is called "witnessing" and people who know God are in public places doing it all the time! Indeed, this is God nudging you and speaking to you, and drawing you in to Himself even before you knew Him. He knows us before we know Him.[27]

Here's something very important for you to remain mindful of if you've begun this process much later in life (after 12yrs old), or after having gone through a lot of heartache/trauma in life: if you were raised by people/a person who did not know God, or if you were surrounded by people who did not know God or, in either case, those who did not believe in God, it's possible they have led you in the wrong way, either through poor guidance, or the lack thereof, or even through very unGodly examples. It's okay.

Please ask God for help to forgive them for these actions and behaviors. Be patient with it, forgiveness might happen slowly, but it will happen. Perhaps they just didn't know how to get to this place that you have now found. Here's the good news: now you know and you can make the right decisions from this point forward. You now have the amazing opportunity to be a good Godly example to those around you and to take responsibility for getting your life back on track. Thank God for that. With God's help you can do all things through Christ Jesus who will give you the strength to do it!

God loves you. That's why He allowed you to be here. With His help you *can* conquer sin and get free of the sin nature. Know this: there is no sin that you cannot overcome and be delivered from. NONE! God desires to help you every step of the way. God thinks very highly of you, no matter how ugly your sin is. God loves you![28]

Finding God is so simple a child can understand. And many do. Find Him today. Love Him forever. And obey Him with your whole heart. It will be worth it.[29]

A Prayer of Salvation

Lord God, I confess that you sent Your Son Jesus to die for me and pardon my sin so that I might be saved. Lord Jesus, I confess with my mouth that you are the only begotten Son of The Living God who has come in the flesh. The only One who can wash away my sin. Thank you for taking my place and reconciling me back unto God our Father. God, I believe in my heart that You raised Jesus from the dead, a death that He did not deserve, yet He surrendered to for me. Right now, in the Name of Jesus, I receive the gift of salvation for my life! Thank You God for Your grace unto me. As it is written, because I believe I am now the righteousness of God, and through my confession I AM SAVED and I know I will not be put to shame!!!! Please God, forgive me of my sins and thank you for saving me from sin, death, and the grave. I want to live for you forever. I will not be ashamed of who You are in my life. I repent of my sins and I receive Your mighty forgiveness right now God, in Jesus' Name. Help me, Most gracious God, please send Your Holy Spirit to live in me, and to show me the way every day for the rest of my life. I welcome you into my body, and mind, and life, and heart, and soul, and spirit Holy Spirit of God. Please be my Comforter and my eternal guide, in Jesus' Name. And I declare by Faith in the Name of Jesus Christ, Yeshua Hamashiach, that I AM SAVED!!!! Amen.[30]

footnotes

#	Pentateuch (Old Testament)	Written Torah (Old Testament)	New Testament
1	Genesis 1:26-27	Psalm 8:5-6	John 1:1-5 Mark 10:6
2		Proverbs 22:15	Romans 7:18-20
3	Genesis 4:5-7		Romans 8:5-8, 12:1-2
4		I Samuel 3:1, 7	John 1:10-12
5		Jeremiah 1:4-7	Ephesians 1:3-6
6	Leviticus 11:44, 19:2	Psalm 51:5	John 8:24 I Peter 1:16
7		Psalm 51:3-6	Romans 7:21 I Corinthians 6:9-11
8	Genesis 8:21		James 4:7-10
9		Proverbs 10:1	Romans 8:1
10		Proverbs 1:7-9, 2:1-5, 22:6	Ephesians 6:4
11		II Chronicles 7:14	John 10:9
12		Isaiah 53:5	John 14:6-7
13	Deuteronomy 30:10-14		Romans 10:8-11

#	Pentateuch (Old Testament)	Written Torah (Old Testament)	New Testament
14		Ezekiel 18:30-32	Luke 13:1-5
15		READ II Samuel 12:9-14	James 1:13-16, 5:16
16		Psalm 32:5-6a	Galatians 1:3-5
17		Zechariah 1:3	Romans 7:23-24
18		Psalm 44:20-21	I John 1:8, 10
19	Leviticus 26:40-42		Revelation 12:10-12
20		Psalm 139:23-24	Mark 7:20-23
21	Exodus 31:3	Psalm 26:2, 51:9-13 Job 32:7-8 Isaiah 61:1-3	II Timothy 1:6-7
22		Proverbs 2:6-12	I John 3:20-21
23		Jeremiah 17:9-10	Mark 7:18-19
24	Leviticus 5:5, 10b, 16b-17, 18b		I John 1:9
25	Exodus 13:14		III John 2-4

#	Pentateuch (Old Testament)	Written Torah (Old Testament)	New Testament
26		READ I Samuel 3:1-10	Hebrews 8:10-12
27		Jeremiah 7:25	John 15:16 Ephesians 1:4-6
28		II Samuel 22:32-33	John 3:14-18
29	Exodus 19:5-6		Galatians 3:27-29
30		Psalm 91:14-16	Romans 10:9-10 Ephesians 2:8

If you have just found God and decided to accept Jesus Christ as your personal Savior and would like additional resources such as prayer, help finding a church, or a listening ear, wherever you are in the United States send an email to:

CounsellnLove@outlook.com

www.ingramcontent.com/pod-product-compliance
Lightning Source LLC
Chambersburg PA
CBHW070457290526
45791CB00005B/2141